Presented to

_____

By

_____

On the Occasion of

_____

Date

_____

PROMISES
of the
PSALMS

*Taste and See
that the Lord Is Good!*

Compiled by
Ellen W. Caughey

BARBOUR
PUBLISHING, INC.
Uhrichsville, Ohio

©MCMXCVII by Barbour Publishing, Inc.

ISBN 1-57748-077-5

All Scripture has been taken from the King James Version of the Bible.

Published by Barbour Publishing, Inc.
            P.O. Box 719
            Uhrichsville, OH 44683
            http:\\www.barbourbooks.com

ecpa   Member of the
       Evangelical Christian
       Publishers Association

Published in the United States of America.

Contents

Introduction

The Lord is faithful to all his promises and loving toward all he has made.   *Psalm 145:13b,* NIV

And what promises await in the Book of Psalms!

Perhaps nowhere else in the Bible are written such comforting words, perhaps nowhere else is the greatness of our God extolled so magnificently. These divinely inspired verses illuminate the character of God with hauntingly beautiful images that will never leave you, lyrical pictures that will be forever painted on your heart.

Come into the sanctuary of God's green pastures. . .rest under the shadow of His wings. . .enter into His gates of thanksgiving. . .realize the strength of His hills, the work of His fingers. Come to be refreshed and renewed by God's promises, loving words that can become the "songs in the house of your pilgrimage,"* a journey that leads to heaven.

See Psalm 119:54.

To my mother,
whose faith in God,
and me,
has never wavered

Angels

The angel of the Lord
encampeth round about them
that fear him,
and delivereth them.

Psalm 34:7

What is man, that thou art mindful of him?. . .For thou hast made him a little lower than the angels, and hast crowned him with glory and honour. *Psalm 8:4, 5*

And the heavens shall praise thy wonders, O LORD: thy faithfulness also in the congregation of the saints. For who in the heaven can be compared unto the LORD? who among the sons of the mighty can be likened unto the LORD? *Psalm 89:5, 6*

Because thou hast made the LORD, which is my refuge, even the most High, thy habitation; there shall no evil befall thee. . .For he shall give his angels charge over thee, to keep thee in all thy ways. They shall bear thee up in their hands, lest thou dash thy foot against a stone. *Psalm 91:9-12*

Bless the LORD, ye his angels, that excel in strength, that do his commandments, hearkening unto the voice of his word. *Psalm 103:20*

Bless the LORD, O my soul. O LORD my God, thou art very great. . .Who maketh his angels spirits; his ministers a flaming fire. *Psalm 104:1, 4*

Anger, the Lord's

Sing unto the Lord,
O ye saints of his, and give thanks at
the remembrance of his holiness.
For his anger endureth but a moment;
in his favour is life:
weeping may endure for a night,
but joy cometh in the morning.
Psalm 30:4, 5

O LORD, rebuke me not in thine anger, neither chasten me in thy hot displeasure. . . .The LORD hath heard my supplication; the LORD will receive my prayer.

Psalm 6:1, 9

God judgeth the righteous, and God is angry with the wicked every day.   *Psalm 7:11*

The LORD trieth the righteous: but the wicked and him that loveth violence his soul hateth. Upon the wicked he shall rain snares, fire and brimstone, and an horrible tempest: this shall be the portion of their cup. For the righteous LORD loveth righteousness; his countenance doth behold the upright.   *Psalm 11:5-7*

Then the earth shook and trembled; the foundations also of the hills moved and were shaken, because he was wroth.   *Psalm 18:7*

God shall hear, and afflict them, even he that abideth of old. Selah. Because they have no changes, therefore they fear not God. . . .But thou, O God, shalt bring them down into the pit of destruction: bloody and deceitful men shall not live out half their days; but I will trust in thee.   *Psalm 55:19, 23*

The LORD is merciful and gracious,
slow to anger,
and plenteous in mercy.
He will not always chide:
neither will he keep his anger for ever
He hath not dealt with us
after our sins; nor rewarded us
according to our iniquities.
Psalm 103:8-10

Until I went into the sanctuary of God; then understood I their end. Surely thou didst set them in slippery places: thou castedst them down into destruction. How are they brought into desolation, as in a moment! they are utterly consumed with terrors. As a dream when one awaketh; so, O LORD, when thou awakest, thou shalt despise their image.   *Psalm 73:17-20*

For, lo, they that are far from thee shall perish: thou hast destroyed all them that go a whoring from thee.
                                                    Psalm 73:27

At thy rebuke, O God of Jacob, both the chariot and horse are cast into a dead sleep. Thou, even thou, art to be feared: and who may stand in thy sight when once thou art angry? Thou didst cause judgment to be heard from heaven; the earth feared, and was still.
                                                    Psalm 76:6-8

Thou hast set our iniquities before thee, our secret sins in the light of thy countenance. For all our days are passed away in thy wrath: we spend our years as a tale that is told. Who knoweth the power of thine anger? even according to thy fear, so is thy wrath.
                                                    Psalm 90:8, 9, 11

The LORD is gracious, and full of compassion; slow to anger, and of great mercy. The LORD is good to all: and his tender mercies are over all his works.

Psalm 145:8, 9

Belief
(Trust in the Lord)

The Lord is
the portion of mine inheritance
and of my cup:
thou maintainest my lot.
I have set the Lord
always before me:
because he is at my right hand,
I shall not be moved.

Psalm 16:5, 8

For the LORD knoweth the way of the righteous: but the way of the ungodly shall perish.   *Psalm 1:6*

I laid me down and slept; I awaked; for the LORD sustained me.   *Psalm 3:5*

But let all those that put their trust in thee rejoice; let them ever shout for joy, because thou defendest them: let them also that love thy name be joyful in thee.
Psalm 5:11

And they that know thy name will put their trust in thee: for thou, LORD, hast not forsaken them that seek thee.
Psalm 9:10

The LORD is my rock, and my fortress, and my deliverer; my God, my strength, in whom I will trust; my buckler, and the horn of my salvation, and my high tower.
Psalm 18:2

The LORD is my shepherd; I shall not want. He maketh me to lie down in green pastures: he leadeth me beside the still waters. He restoreth my soul: he leadeth me in the paths of righteousness for his name's sake.
Psalm 23: 1-3

O taste and see
that the Lord is good:
blessed is the man
that trusteth in him.
Psalm 34:8

He shall receive the blessing from the LORD, and righteousness from the God of his salvation. This is the generation of them that seek him, that seek thy face, O Jacob. Selah.   *Psalm 24:5, 6*

Yea, let none that wait on thee be ashamed: let them be ashamed which transgress without cause. *Psalm 25:3*

All the paths of the LORD are mercy and truth unto such as keep his covenant and his testimonies.
                              Psalm 25:10

The secret of the LORD is with them that fear him; and he will shew them his covenant.   *Psalm 25:14*

Many sorrows shall be to the wicked: but he that trusteth in the LORD, mercy shall compass him about.
                              Psalm 32:10

Fret not thyself because of evildoers, neither be thou envious against the workers of iniquity. For they shall soon be cut down like the grass, and wither as the green herb. Trust in the LORD, and do good; so shalt thou dwell in the land, and verily thou shalt be fed.   *Psalm 37:1-3*

Delight thyself also in the LORD; and he shall give thee the desires of thine heart. Commit thy way unto the LORD; trust also in him; and he shall bring it to pass. And he shall bring forth thy righteousness as the light, and thy judgment as the noonday.   *Psalm 37:4-6*

And he hath put a new song in my mouth, even praise unto our God: many shall see it, and fear, and shall trust in the LORD.   *Psalm 40:3*

Sacrifice and offering thou didst not desire; mine ears hast thou opened: burnt-offering and sin-offering hast thou not required. Then said I, Lo, I come: in the volume of the book it is written of me.   *Psalm 40:6, 7*

But I am like a green olive tree in the house of God: I trust in the mercy of God for ever and ever.
                                          Psalm 52:8

What time I am afraid, I will trust in thee.
                                          Psalm 56:3

I will cry unto God most high; unto God that performeth all things for me.   *Psalm 57:2*

For a day in thy courts
is better than a thousand.
I had rather be a doorkeeper
in the house of my God,
than to dwell in
the tents of wickedness.
For the Lord God is a sun and shield:
the Lord will give
grace and glory:
no good thing will he withhold
from them that walk uprightly.
O Lord of hosts,
blessed is the man
that trusteth in thee.
Psalm 84:10-12

Trust in him at all times; ye people, pour out your heart before him: God is a refuge for us. Selah.   *Psalm 62:8*

Blessed are they that dwell in thy house: they will be still praising thee. Selah. Blessed is the man whose strength is in thee; in whose hearts are the ways of them.   *Psalm 84:4, 5*

Because he hath set his love upon me [God], therefore will I deliver him: I will set him on high, because he hath known my name. He shall call upon me, and I will answer him: I will be with him in trouble; I will deliver him, and honour him. With long life will I satisfy him, and shew him my salvation.   *Psalm 91:14-16*

Those that be planted in the house of the LORD shall flourish in the courts of our God. They shall still bring forth fruit in old age; they shall be fat and flourishing.
                                              Psalm 92:13, 14

Ye that love the LORD, hate evil: he preserveth the souls of his saints; he delivereth them out of the hand of the wicked. Light is sown for the righteous, and gladness for the upright in heart.   *Psalm 97:10, 11*

He shall not be afraid of evil tidings: his heart is fixed, trusting in the LORD. *Psalm 112:7*

Blessed be he that cometh in the name of the LORD.
Psalm 118:26a

The LORD is thy keeper: the LORD is thy shade upon thy right hand. The sun shall not smite thee by day, nor the moon by night. The LORD shall preserve thee from all evil: he shall preserve thy soul. The LORD shall preserve thy going out and thy coming in from this time forth, and even for evermore. *Psalm 121:5-8*

They that trust in the LORD shall be as mount Zion, which cannot be removed, but abideth for ever.
Psalm 125:1

Blessed is every one that feareth the LORD; that walketh in his ways. For thou shalt eat the labour of thine hands: happy shalt thou be, and it shall be well with thee.
Psalm 128:1, 2

For he is our God;
and we are the people
of his pasture,
and the sheep of his hand.
To day if ye will hear his voice,
harden not your heart,
as in the provocation,
and as in the day of
temptation in the wilderness.
Psalm 95:7, 8

How shall we sing the LORD's song in a strange land? If I forget thee, O Jerusalem, let my right hand forget her cunning. If I do not remember thee, let my tongue cleave to the roof of my mouth; if I prefer not Jerusalem above my chief joy.   *Psalm 137:4-6*

Cause me to hear thy lovingkindness in the morning; for in thee do I trust: cause me to know the way wherein I should walk; for I lift up my soul unto thee.
                                                Psalm 143:8

The LORD preserveth all them that love him: but all the wicked will he destroy.   *Psalm 145:20*

He delighteth not in the strength of the horse: he taketh not pleasure in the legs of a man. The LORD taketh pleasure in them that fear him, in those that hope in his mercy.   *Psalm 147:10, 11*

Creation
of the World,
by God

By the word of the Lord
were the heavens made;
and all the host of them
by the breath of his mouth.
For he spake, and it was done;
he commanded, and it stood fast.
Psalm 33:6, 9

When I consider thy heavens, the work of thy fingers, the moon and the stars, which thou hast ordained; what is man, that thou art mindful of him?   *Psalm 8:3, 4a*

Yea, he sent out his arrows, and scattered them; and he shot out lightnings, and discomfited them. Then the channels of waters were seen, and the foundations of the world were discovered at thy rebuke, O LORD, at the blast of the breath of thy nostrils.   *Psalm 18:14, 15*

The heavens declare the glory of God; and the firmament sheweth his handywork.   *Psalm 19:1*

The earth is the LORD's, and the fulness thereof; the world, and they that dwell therein. For he hath founded it upon the seas, and established it upon the floods.
                                              Psalm 24:1, 2

The mighty God, even the LORD, hath spoken, and called the earth from the rising of the sun unto the going down thereof. Out of Zion, the perfection of beauty, God hath shined.   *Psalm 50:1, 2*

The day is thine, the night also is thine: thou hast prepared the light and the sun. Thou hast set all the borders of the earth: thou hast made summer and winter.

Psalm 74:16, 17

The heavens are thine, the earth also is thine: as for the world and the fulness thereof, thou hast founded them. *Psalm 89:11*

Before the mountains were brought forth, or ever thou hadst formed the earth and the world, even from everlasting to everlasting, thou art God. For a thousand years in thy sight are but as yesterday when it is past, and as a watch in the night. *Psalm 90:2, 4*

The floods have lifted up, O LORD, the floods have lifted up their voice; the floods lift up their waves. The LORD on high is mightier than the noise of many waters, yea, than the mighty waves of the sea.

Psalm 93:3, 4

For the Lord is a great God, and a great King above all gods. In his hand are the deep places of the earth: the strength of the hills is his also. The sea is his, and he made it: and his hands formed the dry land. *Psalm 95:3-5*

Thy kingdom is
an everlasting kingdom,
and thy dominion endureth
throughout all generations.
Psalm 145:13

For all the gods of the nations are idols: but the Lord made the heavens. *Psalm 96:5*

Of old hast thou laid the foundation of the earth: and the heavens are the work of thy hands. But thou art the same, and thy years shall have no end.

Psalm 102:25, 27

Who laid the foundations of the earth, that it should not be removed for ever. O Lord, how manifold are thy works! in wisdom hast thou made them all: the earth is full of thy riches. *Psalm 104:5, 24*

For ever, O LORD, thy word is settled in heaven. Thy faithfulness is unto all generations: thou hast established the earth, and it abideth. *Psalm 119:89, 90*

I will lift up mine eyes unto the hills, from whence cometh my help. My help cometh from the LORD, which made heaven and earth. *Psalm 121:1, 2*

Whatsoever the LORD pleased, that did he in heaven, and in earth, in the seas, and all deep places. He causeth the vapours to ascend from the ends of the earth; he maketh lightnings for the rain; he bringeth the wind out of his treasuries.   *Psalm 135:6, 7*

O give thanks unto the LORD; for he is good: for his mercy endureth for ever. To him that by wisdom made the heavens: for his mercy endureth for ever. To him that stretched out the earth above the waters: for his mercy endureth for ever. To him that made great lights: for his mercy endureth for ever: The sun to rule by day: for his mercy endureth for ever: The moon and stars to rule by night: for his mercy endureth for ever.

Psalm 136:1, 5-9

He telleth the number of the stars; he calleth them all by their names. Great is our LORD, and of great power: his understanding is infinite.

Psalm 147:4, 5

Death

For this God is
our God for ever and ever:
he will be our guide
even unto death.
Psalm 48:14

Return, O LORD, deliver my soul: oh save me for thy mercies' sake. For in death there is no remembrance of thee: in the grave who shall give thee thanks?   *Psalm 6:4, 5*

Yea, though I walk through the valley of the shadow of death, I will fear no evil: for thou art with me; thy rod and thy staff they comfort me.   *Psalm 23:4*

O LORD my God, I cried unto thee, and thou hast healed me. O LORD, thou hast brought up my soul from the grave: thou hast kept me alive, that I should not go down to the pit.   *Psalm 30:2, 3*

Behold, the eye of the LORD is upon them that fear him, upon them that hope in his mercy; to deliver their soul from death, and to keep them alive in famine.
Psalm 33:18, 19

For he seeth that wise men die, likewise the fool and the brutish person perish, and leave their wealth to others. Their inward thought is, that their houses shall continue for ever, and their dwelling places to all generations; they call their lands after their own names. Nevertheless man being in honour abideth not: he is like the beasts that perish. But God will redeem my soul from the power of the grave: for he shall receive me. Selah. *Psalm 49:10-12, 15*

He that is our God is the God of salvation; and unto God the LORD belong the issues from death. *Psalm 68:20*

What man is he that liveth, and shall not see death? shall he deliver his soul from the hand of the grave? Selah.
Psalm 89:48

The sorrows of death compassed me, and the pains of hell gat hold upon me: I found trouble and sorrow. Then called I upon the name of the LORD; O LORD, I beseech thee, deliver my soul. Gracious is the LORD, and righteous; yea, our God is merciful. *Psalm 116:3-5*

Precious in the sight of the LORD is the death of his saints. *Psalm 116:15*

Eternal Life
(the gift of Salvation)

As for me,
I will behold thy
face in righteousness:
I shall be satisfied,
when I awake,
with thy likeness.
Psalm 17:15

Salvation belongeth unto the LORD: thy blessing is upon thy people. Selah.   *Psalm 3:8*

For thou wilt not leave my soul in hell; neither wilt thou suffer thine Holy One to see corruption. Thou wilt shew me the path of life: in thy presence is fulness of joy; at thy right hand there are pleasures for evermore.
Psalm 16:10, 11

Thou hast also given me the shield of thy salvation: and thy right hand hath holden me up, and thy gentleness hath made me great.   *Psalm 18:35*

Surely goodness and mercy shall follow me all the days of my life: and I will dwell in the house of the LORD for ever.   *Psalm 23:6*

The LORD is my light and my salvation; whom shall I fear? the LORD is the strength of my life; of whom shall I be afraid?   *Psalm 27:1*

One thing have I desired of the LORD, that will I seek after; that I may dwell in the house of the LORD all the days of my life, to behold the beauty of the LORD, and to enquire in his temple.   *Psalm 27:4*

O LORD, thou hast brought up my soul from the grave: thou hast kept me alive, that I should not go down to the pit.   *Psalm 30:3*

For with thee is the fountain of life: in thy light shall we see light.   *Psalm 36:9*

The LORD knoweth the days of the upright: and their inheritance shall be for ever.   *Psalm 37:18*

But the salvation of the righteous is of the LORD: he is their strength in the time of trouble. And the LORD shall help them, and deliver them: he shall deliver them from the wicked, and save them, because they trust in him.
                                        Psalm 37:39, 40

For thou hast delivered my soul from death: wilt not thou deliver my feet from falling, that I may walk before God in the light of the living?   *Psalm 56:13*

But God will redeem
my soul from
the power of the grave:
for he shall receive me.
Selah.
Psalm 49:15

Truly my soul waiteth upon God: from him cometh my salvation. He only is my rock and my salvation; he is my defence; I shall not be greatly moved.

Psalm 62:1, 2

Thou shalt guide me with thy counsel, and afterward receive me to glory. Whom have I in heaven but thee? and there is none upon earth that I desire beside thee. My flesh and my heart faileth: but God is the strength of my heart, and my portion for ever.

Psalm 73:24-26

He sent redemption unto his people: he hath commanded his covenant for ever: holy and reverend is his name.   *Psalm 111:9*

I shall not die, but live, and declare the works of the LORD.   *Psalm 118:17*

Salvation is far from the wicked: for they seek not thy statutes.   *Psalm 119:155*

Thy kingdom is an everlasting kingdom, and thy dominion endureth throughout all generations.

Psalm 145:13

Family

A father of the fatherless,
and a judge of the widows,
is God in his
holy habitation.
God setteth the solitary
in families:
he bringeth out those
which are bound with chains:
but the rebellious dwell
in a dry land.
Psalm 68:5, 6

Our fathers trusted in thee: they trusted, and thou didst deliver them. They cried unto thee, and were delivered: they trusted in thee, and were not confounded.

Psalm 22:4

A seed shall serve him; it shall be accounted to the Lord for a generation. They shall come, and shall declare his righteousness unto a people that shall be born, that he hath done this.

Psalm 22:30, 31

Remember not the sins of my youth, nor my transgressions: according to thy mercy remember thou me for thy goodness' sake, O LORD.

Psalm 25:7

When my father and my mother forsake me, then the LORD will take me up.

Psalm 27:10

For thou, O God, hast heard my vows: thou hast given me the heritage of those that fear thy name.

Psalm 61:5

For thou art my hope, O Lord GOD: thou art my trust from my youth. By thee have I been holden up from the womb: thou art he that took me out of my mother's bowels: my praise shall be continually of thee.

Psalm 71:5, 6

O God, thou hast taught me from my youth: and hither-to have I declared thy wondrous works. Now also when I am old and greyheaded, O God, forsake me not; until I have shewed thy strength unto this generation, and thy power to every one that is to come. *Psalm 71:17, 18*

We will not hide them from their children, shewing to the generation to come the praises of the LORD, and his strength, and his wonderful works that he hath done. For he established a testimony in Jacob, and appointed a law in Israel, which he commanded our fathers, that they should make them known to their children: that the generation to come might know them, even the children which should be born; who should arise and declare them to their children: that they might set their hope in God, and not forget the works of God, but keep his com-mandments.   *Psalm 78:4-7*

Like as a father pitieth his children, so the LORD pitieth them that fear him. For he knoweth our frame; he re-membereth that we are dust.   *Psalm 103:13, 14*

Praise ye the LORD. Blessed is the man that feareth the LORD, that delighteth greatly in his commandments. His seed shall be mighty upon the earth: the generation of the upright shall be blessed.   *Psalm 112:1, 2*

But the mercy of the Lord
is from everlasting to everlasting
upon them that fear him,
and his righteousness
unto children's children;
to such as keep his covenant,
and to those that remember
his commandments to do them.
Psalm 103:17, 18

He maketh the barren woman to keep house, and to be a joyful mother of children. Praise ye the LORD.

Psalm 113:9

He will bless them that fear the LORD, both small and great. The LORD shall increase you more and more, you and your children. Ye are blessed of the LORD which made heaven and earth. The heaven, even the heavens, are the LORD's: but the earth hath he given to the children of men.

Psalm 115:13-16

Except the Lord build the house, they labour in vain that build it: . . .It is vain for you to rise up early, to sit up late, to eat the bread of sorrows: for so he giveth his beloved sheep.

Psalm 127:1a, 2

Lo, children are an heritage of the LORD: and the fruit of the womb is his reward. As arrows are in the hand of a mighty man; so are children of the youth. Happy is the man that hath his quiver full of them: they shall not be ashamed, but they shall speak with the enemies in the gate.

Psalm 127:3-5

Blessed is every one that feareth the LORD; that walketh in his ways. . . .Thy wife shall be as a fruitful vine by the sides of thine house: thy children like olive plants round about thy table. *Psalm 128:1, 3*

That our sons may be as plants grown up in their youth; that our daughters may be as corner stones, polished after the similitude of a palace:. . . Happy is that people, that is in such a case: yea, happy is that people, whose God is the Lord. *Psalm 144:12, 15*

One generation shall praise thy works to another, and shall declare thy mighty acts. *Psalm 145:4*

God's Greatness

The Lord is in his holy temple,
the Lord's throne is in heaven:
his eyes behold,
his eyelids try,
the children of men.
Psalm 11:4

O LORD, our LORD, how excellent is thy name in all the earth! who hast set thy glory above the heavens. . . . When I consider thy heavens, the work of thy fingers, the moon and the stars, which thou hast ordained; What is man, that thou art mindful of him?. . . .

Psalm 8:1, 3, 4

Yea, he sent out his arrows, and scattered them; and he shot out lightnings, and discomfited them. Then the channels of waters were seen, and the foundations of the world were discovered at thy rebuke, O LORD, at the blast of the breath of thy nostrils.   *Psalm 18:14, 15*

The heavens declare the glory of God; and the firmament sheweth his handywork. Day unto day uttereth speech, and night unto night sheweth knowledge. There is no speech nor language, where their voice is not heard.   *Psalm 19:1-3*

In them hath he set a tabernacle for the sun, which is as a bridegroom coming out of his chamber, and rejoiceth as a strong man to run a race. His going forth is from the end of the heaven, and his circuit unto the ends of it: and there is nothing hid from the heat thereof.

Psalm 19:4b-6

All the ends of the world shall remember and turn unto the LORD: and all the kindreds of the nations shall worship before thee. For the kingdom is the LORD's: and he is the governor among the nations.

Psalm 22:27, 28

The earth is the LORD's, and the fulness thereof; the world, and they that dwell therein. For he hath founded it upon the seas, and established it upon the floods.

Psalm 24:1, 2

Give unto the LORD the glory due unto his name; worship the LORD in the beauty of holiness. The voice of the LORD is upon the waters: the God of glory thundereth: the LORD is upon many waters. The voice of the LORD is powerful; the voice of the LORD is full of majesty.

Psalm 29:2-4

The Lord sitteth upon the flood; yea, the Lord sitteth King for ever. *Psalm 29:10*

Oh how great is thy goodness, which thou hast laid up for them that fear thee: which thou hast wrought for them that trust in thee before the sons of men!

Psalm 31:19

For who is God
save the LORD?
or who is a rock
save our God?
It is God that
girdeth me with strength,
and maketh my way perfect.
He maketh my feet
ike hinds' feet,
and setteth me upon
my high places.
Psalm 18:31-33

By the word of the LORD were the heavens made; and all the host of them by the breath of his mouth. He gathereth the waters of the sea together as an heap: he layeth up the depth in storehouses. Let all the earth fear the LORD: let all the inhabitants of the world stand in awe of him. For he spake, and it was done; he commanded, and it stood fast.   *Psalm 33:6-9*

The LORD looketh from heaven; he beholdeth all the sons of men. From the place of his habitation he looketh upon all the inhabitants of the earth. He fashioneth their hearts alike; he considereth all their works.

Psalm 33:13-15

Come, behold the works of the LORD. . .He maketh wars to cease unto the end of the earth; he breaketh the bow, and cutteth the spear in sunder; he burneth the chariot in the fire. Be still, and know that I am God: I will be exalted among the heathen, I will be exalted in the earth.

Psalm 46:8-10

Great is the LORD, and greatly to be praised in the city of our God, in the mountain of his holiness.

Psalm 48:1

The mighty God, even the LORD, hath spoken, and called the earth from the rising of the sun unto the going down thereof. Out of Zion, the perfection of beauty, God hath shined. *Psalm 50:1, 2*

In God have I put my trust: I will not be afraid what man can do unto me. *Psalm 56:11*

O God, thou art my God; early will I seek thee: my soul thirsteth for thee, my flesh longeth for thee in a dry and thirsty land, where no water is; to see thy power and glory, so as I have seen thee in the sanctuary. Because thy lovingkindness is better than life, my lips shall praise thee. *Psalm 63:1-3*

By terrible things in righteousness wilt thou answer us, O God of our salvation; who art the confidence of all the ends of the earth, and of them that are afar off upon the sea. *Psalm 65:5*

Thou visitest the earth, and waterest it: thou greatly enrichest it with the river of God, which is full of water: . . .Thou crownest the year with thy goodness. . . .The pastures are clothed with flocks; the valleys also are covered over with corn; they shout for joy, they also sing. *Psalm 65:9, 11, 13*

Many, O Lord my God,
are thy wonderful works
which thou has done,
and thy thoughts
which are to us-ward:
they cannot be reckoned up
in order unto thee:
if I would declare
and speak of them,
they are more than
can be numbered.
Psalm 40:5

Sing unto God, ye kingdoms of the earth. . .to him that rideth upon the heavens of heavens, which were of old; lo, he doth send out his voice, and that a mighty voice.
Psalm 68:32, 33

Thy righteousness also, O God, is very high, who hast done great things: O God, who is like unto thee!
Psalm 71:19

The day is thine, the night also is thine: thou hast prepared the light and the sun. Thou hast set all the borders of the earth: thou hast made summer and winter.
Psalm 74:16, 17

Thy way, O God, is in the sanctuary: who is so great a God as our God? Thou art the God that doest wonders. . . .
Psalm 77:13, 14

The voice of thy thunder was in the heaven: the lightnings lightened the world: the earth trembled and shook. Thy way is in the sea, and thy path in the great waters, and thy footsteps are not known.
Psalm 77:18, 19

For the LORD God is a sun and shield: the LORD will give grace and glory: no good things will he withhold from them that walk uprightly.   *Psalm 84:11*

Yea, the Lord shall give that which is good. . . Righteousness shall go before him; and shall set us in the way of his steps.   *Psalm 85:12, 13*

Among the gods there is none like unto thee, O LORD; neither are there any works like unto thy works. For thou art great, and doest wondrous things: thou art God alone.   *Psalm 86:8, 10*

The heavens are thine, the earth also is thine: as for the world and the fulness thereof, thou hast founded them.
          Psalm 89:11

Before the mountains were brought forth, or ever thou hadst brought forth, or ever thou hadst formed the earth and the world, even from everlasting to everlasting, thou art God. For a thousand years in thy sight are but as yesterday when it is past, and as a watch in the night.
          Psalm 90:2, 4

His name shall endure for ever:
his name shall be continued
as long as the sun:
and men shall be blessed in him:
all nations shall call him blessed.
Blessed be the Lord God,
the God of Israel,
who only doeth wondrous things.
Psalm 72:17, 18

The LORD reigneth, he is clothed with majesty; the LORD is clothed with strength, wherewith he hath girded himself: the world also is stablished, that it cannot be moved. Thy throne is established of old: thou art from everlasting. *Psalm 93:1, 2*

In his hand are the deep places of the earth: the strength of the hills is his also. *Psalm 95:4*

Make a joyful noise unto the LORD, all ye lands. Serve the LORD with gladness: come before his presence with singing. Know ye that the LORD he is God: it is he that hath made us, and not we ourselves; we are his people, and the sheep of his pasture. *Psalm 100:1-3*

But thou art the same, and thy years shall have no end. *Psalm 102:27*

Bless the LORD, O my soul. O LORD my God, thou art very great; thou art clothed with honour and majesty. Who coverest thyself with light as with a garment: who stretchest out the heavens like a curtain: who layeth the beams of his chambers in the waters: who maketh the clouds his chariot: who walketh upon the wings of the wind. *Psalm 104:1-3*

As the mountains are round about Jerusalem, so the Lord is round about his people from henceforth even for ever. *Psalm 125:2*

Whatsoever the LORD pleased, that did he in heaven, and in earth, in the seas, and all deep places. He causeth the vapours to ascend from the ends of the earth; he maketh lightnings for the rain; he bringeth the wind out of his treasuries. *Psalm 134:6, 7*

O Lord, thou hast searched me, and known me. Thou knowest my downsitting and mine uprising, thou understandest my thought afar off. Thou compassest my path and my lying down, and art acquainted with all my ways. For there is not a word in my tongue, but, lo, O Lord, thou knowest it altogether. *Psalm 139:1-4*

I will praise thee; for I am fearfully and wonderfully made: marvellous are thy works; and that my soul knoweth right well. . .How precious also are thy thoughts unto me, O God! how great is the sum of them! If I should count them, they are more in number than the sand: when I awake, I am still with thee.

Psalm 139:14, 17, 18

The LORD is righteous in all his ways, and holy in all his works. The LORD is nigh unto all them that call upon him, to all that call upon him in truth.

Psalm 145:17, 18

He telleth the number of the stars; he calleth them all by their names. Great is our Lord, and of great power: his understanding is infinite.   *Psalm 147:4, 5*

God's
Justice

Arise, O LORD;
let not man prevail:
let the heathen
be judged in thy sight.
Put them in fear, O LORD:
that the nations
may know themselves
to be but men. Selah.
Psalm 9:19, 20

But know that the LORD hath set apart him that is godly for himself: the LORD will hear when I call unto him.   *Psalm 4:3*

For thou art not a God that hath pleasure in wickedness: neither shall evil dwell with thee.   *Psalm 5:4*

God judgeth the righteous, and God is angry with the wicked every day. If he turn not, he will whet his sword; he hath bent his bow, and made it ready.
                                             Psalm 7:11, 12

The LORD is known by the judgment which he executeth: the wicked is snared in the work of his own hands.   *Psalm 9:16*

The Lord trieth the righteous: but the wicked and him that loveth violence his soul hateth. Upon the wicked he shall rain snares, fire and brimstone, and an horrible tempest: this shall be the portion of their cup. For the righteous Lord loveth righteousness; his countenance doth behold the upright.   *Psalm 11:5-7*

The LORD rewarded me according to my righteousness; according to the cleanness of my hands hath he recompensed me.   *Psalm 18:20*

With the merciful thou wilt shew thyself merciful; with an upright man thou wilt shew thyself upright; with the pure thou wilt shew thyself pure. . .for thou wilt save the afflicted people; but wilt bring down high looks.
                                                          Psalm 18:25-27

The law of the Lord is perfect, converting the soul: the testimony of the Lord is sure, making wise the simple. The statutes of the Lord are right, rejoicing the heart: the commandment of the Lord is pure, enlightening the eyes. The fear of the Lord is clean, enduring for ever: the judgments of the Lord are true and righteous altogether.   *Psalm 19:7-9*

I had fainted, unless I had believed to see the goodness of the LORD in the land of the living. Wait on the LORD: be of good courage, and he shall strengthen thine heart: wait, I say, on the LORD.   *Psalm 27:13, 14*

But the Lord shall
endure for ever:
he hath prepared
his throne for judgment.
And he shall judge
the world in righteousness,
he shall minister judgment
to the people in uprightness.
Psalm 9:7, 8

Thy righteouness is like the great mountains; thy judgments are a great deep: O LORD, thou preservest man and beast.   *Psalm 36:6*

And he shall bring forth thy righteousness as the light, and thy judgment as the noonday.   *Psalm 37:6*

Cease from anger, and forsake wrath: fret not thyself in any wise to do evil. For evildoers shall be cut off: but those that wait upon the LORD, they shall inherit the earth.   *Psalm 37:8, 9*

Thy throne, O God, is for ever and ever: the sceptre of thy kingdom is a right sceptre.   *Psalm 45:6*

Our God shall come, and shall not keep silence: a fire shall devour before him, and it shall be very tempestuous round about him. He shall call to the heavens from above, and to the earth, that he may judge his people. Gather my saints together unto me; those that have made a covenant with me by sacrifice. And the heavens shall declare his righteousness: for God is judge himself. Selah.   *Psalm 50:3-6*

So that a man shall say, Verily there is a reward for the righteous: verily he is a God that judgeth in the earth.

Psalm 58:11

For promotion cometh neither from the east, nor from the west, nor from the south. But God is the judge: he putteth down one, and setteth up another.

Psalm 75:6, 7

Arise, O God, judge the earth: for thou shalt inherit all nations. *Psalm 82:8*

Thou hast a mighty arm: strong is thy hand, and high is thy right hand. Justice and judgment are the habitation of thy throne: mercy and truth shall go before thy face.

Psalm 89:13, 14

Let the field be joyful, and all that is therein: then shall all the trees of the wood rejoice before the LORD: for he cometh, for he cometh to judge the earth: he shall judge the world with righteousness, and the people with his truth. *Psalm 96:12, 13*

The works of his hands are verity and judgment; all his commandments are sure. They stand fast for ever and ever, and are done in truth and uprightness.

Psalm 111:7, 8

God's Mercy and Love

Many sorrows shall
be to the wicked:
but he that trusteth in the Lord,
mercy shall compass him about.
Psalm 32:10

But I have trusted in thy mercy; my heart shall rejoice in thy salvation. I will sing unto the LORD, because he hath dealt bountifully with me.   *Psalm 13:5, 6*

I have called upon thee, for thou wilt hear me, O God . . . shew thy marvellous lovingkindness, O thou that savest by thy right hand them which put their trust in thee from those that rise up against them.   *Psalm 17:6, 7*

With the merciful thou wilt shew thyself merciful; with an upright man thou wilt shew thyself upright.
          Psalm 18:25

Surely goodness and mercy shall follow me all the days of my life: and I will dwell in the house of the Lord for ever.   *Psalm 23:6*

All the paths of the LORD are mercy and truth unto such as keep his covenant and his testimonies. For thy name's sake, O LORD, pardon mine iniquity; for it is great.
          Psalm 25:10, 11

Blessed be the LORD, because he hath heard the voice of my supplications.   *Psalm 28:6*

Oh, how great is thy goodness, which thou hast laid up for them that fear thee; which thou hast wrought for them that trust in thee before the sons of men! Thou shalt hide them in the secret of thy presence from the pride of man: thou shalt keep them secretly in a pavilion from the strife of tongues. Blessed be the LORD: for he hath shewed me his marvellous kindness in a strong city.   *Psalm 31:19-21*

For day and night thy hand was heavy upon me: my moisture is turned into the drought of summer. Selah. I acknowledged my sin unto thee, and mine iniquity have I not hid, I said, I will confess my transgressions unto the LORD; and thou forgavest the iniquity of my sin.

Psalm 32:4, 5

Thy mercy, O LORD, is in the heavens; and thy faithfulness reacheth unto the clouds.   *Psalm 36:5*

The steps of a good man are ordered by the LORD: and he delighteth in his way. Though he fall, he shall not be utterly cast down: for the LORD upholdeth him with his hand.   *Psalm 37:23, 24*

If we have forgotten
the name of our God,
or stretched out our hands
to a strange god;
shall not God search this out?
for he knoweth the secrets
of the heart.
Psalm 44:20, 21

I have been young, and now am old; yet have I not seen the righteous forsaken, nor his seed begging bread. He is ever merciful, and lendeth; and his seed is blessed.   *Psalm 37:25, 26*

I waited patiently for the LORD; and he inclined unto me, and heard my cry. He brought me up also out of an horrible pit, out of the miry clay, and set my feet upon a rock, and established my goings. And he hath put a new song in my mouth, even praise unto our God: many shall see it, and fear, and shall trust in the LORD.

Psalm 40:1-3

Yet the LORD will command his lovingkindness in the daytime, and in the night his song shall be with me, and my prayer unto the God of my life.

Psalm 42:8

For thy mercy is great unto the heavens, and thy truth unto the clouds.   *Psalm 57:10*

Because thy lovingkindness is better than life, my lips shall praise thee.   *Psalm 63:3*

Blessed be God, which hath not turned away my prayer, nor his mercy from me. *Psalm 66:20*

O God, thou knowest my foolishness; and my sins are not hid from thee. *Psalm 69:5*

Surely his salvation is nigh them that fear him; that glory may dwell in our land. Mercy and truth are met together; righteousness and peace have kissed each other. *Psalm 85:9*

For thou, Lord, art good, and ready to forgive; and plenteous in mercy unto all them that call upon thee. *Psalm 86:5*

Because he hath set his love upon me, therefore will I deliver him: I will set him on high, because he hath known my name. *Psalm 91:14*

Blessed is the man whom thou chastenest, O LORD, and teachest him out of thy law; that thou mayest give him rest from the days of adversity, until the pit be digged for the wicked. For the LORD will not cast off his people, neither will he forsake his inheritance. *Psalm 94:12-14*

If thou, Lord,
shouldest mark iniquities,
O Lord, who shall stand?
But there is forgiveness with thee,
that thou mayest be feared.
Psalm 130:3, 4

When I said, My foot slippeth; thy mercy, O LORD, held me up. *Psalm 94:18*

Enter into his gates with thanksgiving, and into his courts with praise: be thankful unto him, and bless his name. For the LORD is good; his mercy is everlasting; and his truth endureth to all generations.

Psalm 100:4, 5

As for man, his days are as grass: as a flower of the field, so he flourisheth. For the wind passeth over it, and it is gone; and the place thereof shall know it no more. But the mercy of the LORD is from everlasting to everlasting upon them that fear him, and his righteousness unto children's children. *Psalm 103:15-17*

O praise the LORD, all ye nations: praise him, all ye people. For his merciful kindness is great toward us: and the truth of the LORD endureth for ever. Praise ye the LORD. *Psalm 117:1, 2*

O give thanks unto the Lord; for he is good: because his mercy endureth for ever. *Psalm 118:1*

Look thou upon me, and be merciful unto me, as thou usest to do unto those that love thy name.

Psalm 119:132

Let Israel hope in the LORD: for with the LORD there is mercy, and with him is plenteous redemption. And he shall redeem Israel from all his iniquities.

Psalm 130:7, 8

O give thanks unto the LORD; for he is good: for his mercy endureth for ever. *Psalm 136:1*

The LORD will perfect that which concerneth me: thy mercy, O LORD, endureth for ever: forsake not the works of thine own hands. *Psalm 138:8*

The LORD is good to all: and his tender mercies are over all his works. *Psalm 145:9*

The LORD preserveth all them that love him: but all the wicked will he destroy. *Psalm 145:20*

For as the heaven is high above the earth, so great is his mercy toward them that fear him. As far as the east is from the west, so far hath he removed our transgressions from us. *Psalm 103:11, 12*

God's Word

The words of the LORD
are pure words:
as silver tried in a furnace of earth,
purified seven times.
Thou shalt keep them,
O LORD,
thou shalt preserve them
from this generation for ever.
Psalm 12:6, 7

As for God, his way is perfect: the word of the LORD is tried: he is a buckler to all those that trust in him.
Psalm 18:30

Shew me thy ways, O LORD; teach me thy paths. Lead me in thy truth, and teach me: for thou art the God of my salvation; on thee do I wait all the day.   *Psalm 25:4, 5*

For the word of the LORD is right; and all his works are done in truth. He loveth righteousness and judgment: the earth is full of the goodness of the LORD. By the word of the LORD were the heavens made; and all the host of them by the breath of his mouth. . .The counsel of the LORD standeth for ever, the thoughts of his heart to all generations.   *Psalm 33:4-6, 11*

In God I will praise his word, in God I have put my trust; I will not fear what flesh can do unto me. In God will I praise his word: in the LORD will I praise his word. In God have I put my trust: I will not be afraid what man can do unto me.   *Psalm 56:4, 10, 11*

God hath spoken once; twice have I heard this; that power belongeth unto God. Also unto thee, O LORD, belongeth mercy: for thou renderest to every man according to his work.   *Psalm 62:11, 12*

My covenant will I not break, nor alter the thing that is gone out of my lips. *Psalm 89:34*

He hath remembered his covenant for ever, the word which he commanded to a thousand generations.
Psalm 105:8

Blessed are the undefiled in the way, who walk in the law of the LORD. Blessed are they that keep his testimonies, and that seek him with the whole heart.
Psalm 119:1, 2

Wherewithal shall a young man cleanse his way? by taking heed thereto according to thy word.
Psalm 119:9

Thy word have I hid in mine heart, that I might not sin against thee. *Psalm 119:11*

I have chosen the way of truth: thy judgments have I laid before me. *Psalm 119:30*

The Lord gave the word:
great was the company
of those that published it.
Psalm 68:11

———⊲≪≫⊳———

Teach me, O LORD, the way of thy statutes; and I shall keep it unto the end. *Psalm 119:33*

Thy statutes have been my songs in the house of my pilgrimage. I have remembered thy name, O LORD, in the night, and have kept thy law.

Psalm 119:54, 55

For ever, O LORD, thy word is settled in heaven. Thy faithfulness is unto all generations: thou hast established the earth, and it abideth. *Psalm 119:89, 90*

Thy word is a lamp unto my feet, and light unto my path. *Psalm 119:105*

Thou art my hiding place and my shield: I hope in thy word. *Psalm 119:114*

The entrance of thy words giveth light; it giveth understanding unto the simple. *Psalm 119:130*

Thou art near, O LORD; and all thy commandments are truth. Concerning thy testimonies, I have known of old that thou hast founded them for ever.

Psalm 119:151, 152

Thy word is true from the beginning: and every one of thy righteous judgments endureth for ever.

Psalm 119:160

I will worship toward thy holy temple, and praise thy name for thy lovingkindness and for thy truth: for thou hast magnified thy word above all thy name.

Psalm 138:2

Gossip

Lord, who shall abide in thy tabernacle?
who shall dwell in thy holy hill?
He that walketh uprightly
and worketh righteousness,
and speaketh the truth in his heart.
He that backbiteth not with his tongue,
nor doeth evil to his neighbour,
nor taketh up a reproach
against his neighbour.
Psalm 15:1-3

Help, LORD; for the godly man ceaseth; for the faithful fail from among the children of men. They speak vanity every one with his neighbour: with flattering lips and with a double heart do they speak. . . . Who have said, With our tongue will we prevail; our lips are our own; who is lord over us?   *Psalm 12:1, 2, 4*

Hear the right, O LORD, attend unto my cry, give ear unto my prayer, that goeth not out of feigned lips. Thou hast proved mine heart; thou hast visited me in the night; thou hast tried me, and shalt find nothing; I am purposed that my mouth shall not transgress.
Psalm 17:1, 3

Let the words of my mouth, and the meditation of my heart, be acceptable in thy sight, O Lord, my strength, and my redeemer.   *Psalm 19:14*

Let the lying lips be put to silence; which speak grievous things proudly and contemptuously against the righteous.   *Psalm 31:18*

Keep thy tongue from evil, and thy lips from speaking guile.   *Psalm 34:13*

The mouth of the righteous speaketh wisdom, and his tongue talketh of judgment. The law of his God is in his heart; none of his steps shall slide.   *Psalm 37:30, 31*

Thou givest thy mouth to evil, and thy tongue frameth deceit. Thou sittest and speakest against thy brother; thou slanderest thine own mother's son. These things hast thou done, and I [God] kept silence; thou thoughtest that I was altogether such an one as thyself: but I will reprove thee, and set them in order before thine eyes.
Psalm 50:19-21

Let my mouth be filled with thy praise and with thy honour all the day.   *Psalm 71:8*

Whoso offereth praise glorifieth me; and to him that ordereth his conversation aright will I shew the salvation of God.   *Psalm 50:23*

Thy tongue deviseth mischiefs; like a sharp razor, working deceitfully.   *Psalm 52:2*

Set a watch, O Lord, before my mouth; keep the door of my lips.   *Psalm 141:3*

Government

Blessed is the nation
whose God is the LORD;
and the people whom he hath
chosen for his own inheritance . . .
There is no king saved by
the multitude of an host:
a mighty man is not
delivered by much strength. . .
Behold, the eye of the LORD
is upon them that fear him,
upon them that hope in his mercy.
Psalm 33:12, 16, 18

Blessed is the man that walketh not in the counsel of the ungodly, nor standeth in the way of sinners, nor sitteth in the seat of the scornful. But his delight is in the law of the LORD; and in his law doth he meditate day and night.   *Psalm 1:1, 2*

Be wise now, therefore, O ye kings: be instructed, ye judges of the earth. Serve the LORD with fear, and rejoice with trembling. Kiss the Son, lest he be angry, and ye perish from the way, when his wrath is kindled but a little. Blessed are all they that put their trust in him.   *Psalm 2:10-12*

The wicked shall be turned into hell, and all nations that forget God. Put them in fear, O LORD: that the nations may know themselves to be but men. Selah.

Psalm 9:17, 20

The king shall joy in thy strength, O LORD; and in thy salvation how greatly shall he rejoice! He asked life of thee, and thou gavest it him, even length of days for ever and ever. His glory is great in thy salvation: honour and majesty hast thou laid upon him. For the king trusteth in the LORD, and through the mercy of the most High he shall not be moved.   *Psalm 21:1, 4, 5, 7*

The LORD bringeth the counsel of the heathen to nought: he maketh the devices of the people of none effect. The counsel of the LORD standeth for ever, the thoughts of his heart to all generations.   *Psalm 32:10, 11*

For I will not trust in my bow, neither shall my sword save me. But thou hast saved us from our enemies, and hast put them to shame that hated us. In God we boast all the day long, and praise thy name for ever. Selah.
Psalm 44:6-8

For God is the King of all the earth: sing ye praises with understanding. God reigneth over the heathen: God sitteth upon the throne of his holiness. The princes of the people are gathered together, even the people of the God of Abraham: for the shields of the earth belong unto God: he is greatly exalted.   *Psalm 47:7-9*

He ruleth by his power for ever; his eyes behold the nations: let not the rebellious exalt themselves. Selah.
Psalm 66:7

It is better to trust in the LORD than to put confidence in man. It is better to trust in the LORD than to put confidence in princes.   *Psalm 118:8, 9*

For all the gods
of the nations
are idols:
but the Lord
made the heavens.
Psalm 96:5

Except the LORD build the house, they labour in vain that build it: except the LORD keep the city, the watchman waketh but in vain. *Psalm 127:1*

For the LORD will judge his people, and he will repent himself concerning his servants. The idols of the heathen are silver and gold, the work of men's hands. They have mouths, but they speak not; eyes have they, but they see not; they have ears, but they hear not; neither is there any breath in their mouths. They that make them are like unto them: so is every one that trusteth in them. *Psalm 135:14-18*

Put not your trust in princes, nor in the son of man, in whom there is no help. His breath goeth forth, he returneth to his earth; in that very day his thoughts perish. *Psalm 146:3, 4*

O let the nations be glad and sing for joy: for thou shalt judge the people righteously, and govern the nations upon earth. Selah. Let the people praise thee, O God: let all the people praise thee. Then shall the earth yield her increase; and God, even our own God, shall bless us. *Psalm 67:4-6*

Help and Comfort in Troubled Times

For thou wilt light my candle:
the Lord my God will
enlighten my darkness.
For by thee I have
run through a troop;
and by my God have
I leaped over a wall.
Psalm 18:28, 29

Many there be which say of my soul, There is no help for him in God. . .But thou, O LORD, art a shield for me; my glory, and the lifter up of mine head. *Psalm 3:2, 3*

The LORD also will be a refuge for the oppressed, a refuge in times of trouble. And they that know thy name will put their trust in thee: for thou, LORD, hast not forsaken them that seek thee. *Psalm 9:9, 10*

The poor committeth himself unto thee; thou art the helper of the fatherless. LORD, thou hast heard the desire of the humble: thou wilt prepare their heart, thou wilt cause thine ear to hear: to judge the fatherless and the oppressed, that the man of the earth may no more oppress. *Psalm 10:14b, 17, 18*

Keep me as the apple of the eye, hide me under the shadow of thy wings, from the wicked that oppress me, from my deadly enemies, who compass me about. *Psalm 17:8, 9*

The sorrows of death compassed me, and the floods of ungodly men made me afraid. The sorrows of hell compassed me about: the snares of death prevented me. *Psalm 18:4, 5*

In my distress I called upon the LORD, and cried unto my God: he heard my voice out of his temple, and my cry came before him, even into his ears.   *Psalm 18:6*

Ye that fear the LORD, praise him; all ye the seed of Jacob, glorify him; and fear him, all ye the seed of Israel. For he hath not despised nor abhorred the affliction of the afflicted; neither hath he hid his face from him; but when he cried unto him, he heard.

Psalm 22:23, 24

Yea, though I walk through the valley of the shadow of death, I will fear no evil: for thou art with me; thy rod and thy staff they comfort me. Thou preparest a table before me in the presence of mine enemies: thou anointest my head with oil; my cup runneth over. Surely goodness and mercy shall follow me all the days of my life: and I will dwell in the house of the LORD for ever.

Psalm 23:4-6

The Lord is my light and my salvation; whom shall I fear? the Lord is the strength of my life; of whom shall I be afraid?   *Psalm 27:1*

The Lord is nigh unto them
that are of a broken heart;
and saveth such as be
of a contrite spirit.
Many are the afflictions
of the righteous:
but the Lord delivereth him
out of them all.
Psalm 34:18, 19

Though an host should encamp against me, my heart shall not fear: though war should rise against me, in this will I be confident. One thing have I desired of the LORD, that will I seek after; that I may dwell in the house of the LORD all the days of my life, to behold the beauty of the LORD, and to enquire in his temple. For in the time of trouble he shall hide me in his pavilion: in the secret of his tabernacle shall he hide me; he shall set me up upon a rock.   *Psalm 27:3-5*

I will be glad and rejoice in thy mercy: for thou hast considered my trouble; thou hast known my soul in adversities; and hast not shut me up into the hand of the enemy: thou hast set my feet in a large room.

Psalm 31:7, 8

I sought the LORD, and he heard me, and delivered me from all my fears. They looked unto him, and were lightened: and their faces were not ashamed.

Psalm 34:4, 5

How excellent is thy lovingkindness, O God! therefore the children of men put their trust under the shadow of thy wings.   *Psalm 36:7*

Blessed is he that considereth the poor: the LORD will deliver him in time of trouble. The LORD will preserve him, and keep him alive; and he shall be blessed upon the earth: and thou wilt not deliver him unto the will of his enemies. The LORD will strengthen him upon the bed of languishing.   *Psalm 41:1-3a*

Why art thou cast down, O my soul? and why art thou disquieted within me? hope thou in God: for I shall yet praise him, who is the health of my countenance, and my God.   *Psalm 42:11*

God is our refuge and strength, a very present help in trouble. Therefore will not we fear, though the earth be removed, and though the mountains be carried into the midst of the sea. Though the waters thereof roar and be troubled, though the mountains shake with the swelling thereof. Selah.   *Psalm 46:1-3*

And call upon me in the day of trouble: I will deliver thee, and thou shalt glorify me.   *Psalm 50:15*

Behold, God is mine helper: the Lord is with them that uphold my soul.   *Psalm 54:4*

He that dwelleth
in the secret place of
the most High
shall abide under the shadow
of the Almighty.
He shall cover thee
with his feathers,
and under his wings
shalt thou trust:
his truth shall be thy
shield and buckler.
Psalm 91:1, 4

As for me, I will call upon God; and the LORD shall save me. Evening, and morning, and at noon, will I pray, and cry aloud: and he shall hear my voice. He hath delivered my soul in peace from the battle that was against me: for there were many with me.   *Psalm 55:16-18*

Cast thy burden upon the LORD, and he shall sustain thee: he shall never suffer the righteous to be moved.
          Psalm 55:22

What time I am afraid, I will trust in thee. *Psalm 56:3*

Thou tellest my wanderings: put thou my tears into thy bottle: are they not in thy book?   *Psalm 56:8*

From the end of the earth will I cry unto thee, when my heart is overwhelmed: lead me to the rock that is higher than I. For thou hast been a shelter for me, and strong tower from the enemy. I will abide in thy tabernacle for ever: I will trust in the covert of thy wings. Selah. For thou, O God, hast heard my vows: thou hast given me the heritage of those that fear thy name.
          Psalm 61:2-5

Though ye have lien among the pots, yet shall ye be as the wings of a dove covered with silver, and her feathers with yellow gold.   *Psalm 68:13*

Thou, which hast shewed me great and sore troubles, shalt quicken me again, and shalt bring me up again from the depths of the earth. Thou shalt increase my greatness, and comfort me on every side.

Psalm 71:20, 21

My flesh and my heart faileth: but God is the strength of my heart, and my portion for ever.   *Psalm 73:26*

I cried unto God with my voice, even unto God with my voice; and he gave ear unto me.   *Psalm 77:1*

In the day of my trouble I will call upon thee: for thou wilt answer me.   *Psalm 86:7*

He shall call upon me, and I will answer him: I will be with him in trouble; I will deliver him, and honour him.

Psalm 91:15

Give ear, O Lord,
unto my prayer:
and attend to the voice
of my supplications.
Psalm 86:6

The LORD preserveth the simple: I was brought low, and he helped me. For thou hast delivered my soul from death, mine eyes from tears, and my feet from falling. I will walk before the LORD in the land of the living.

Psalm 116:6, 8, 9

I called upon the LORD in distress: the LORD answered me, and set me in a large place. The LORD is on my side; I will not fear: what can man do unto me?

Psalm 118:5, 6

This is my comfort in my affliction: for thy word hath quickened me. *Psalm 119:50*

Trouble and anguish have taken hold on me: yet thy commandments are my delights. The righteousness of thy testimonies is everlasting: give me understanding, and I shall live. *Psalm 119:143, 144*

I will lift up mine eyes unto the hills, from whence cometh my help. My help cometh from the LORD, which made heaven and earth. He will not suffer thy foot to be moved: he that keepeth thee will not slumber. Behold, he that keepeth Israel shall neither slumber nor sleep.

Psalm 121:1-4

The LORD is thy keeper: the LORD is thy shade upon thy right hand. The sun shall not smite thee by day, nor the moon by night. The LORD shall preserve thee from all evil: he shall preserve thy soul. the LORD shall preserve thy going out and thy coming in from this time forth, and even for evermore. *Psalm 121:5-8*

Our help is in the name of the LORD, who made heaven and earth. *Psalm 124:8*

As the mountains are round about Jerusalem, so the LORD is round about his people from henceforth even for ever. *Psalm 125:2*

They that sow in tears shall reap in joy. He that goeth forth and weepeth, bearing precious seed, shall doubtless come again with rejoicing, bringing his sheaves with him. *Psalm 126:5, 6*

In the day when I cried thou answeredst me, and strengthenedst me with strength in my soul. Though I walk in the midst of trouble, thou wilt revive me: thou shalt stretch forth thine hand against the wrath of mine enemies, and thy right hand shall save me. *Psalm 138:3, 7*

The Lord is nigh unto
all them that call upon him,
to all that call upon him in truth.
He will fulfil the desire
of them that fear him:
he also will hear their cry,
and will save them.
Psalm 145:18, 19

If I ascend up into heaven, thou art there: if I make my bed in hell, behold, thou art there. If I take the wings of the morning, and dwell in the uttermost parts of the sea; even there shall thy hand lead me, and thy right hand shall hold me. . . . Yea, the darkness hideth not from thee; but the night shineth as the day: the darkness and the light are both alike to thee.

Psalm 139:8-10, 12

When my spirit was overwhelmed within me, then thou knewest my path.   *Psalm 142:3a*

The LORD openeth the eyes of the blind: the LORD raiseth them that are bowed down: the LORD loveth the righteous: the LORD preserveth the strangers; he relieveth the fatherless and widow: but the way of the wicked he turneth upside down.   *Psalm 146:8, 9*

He healeth the broken in heart, and bindeth up their wounds.   *Psalm 147:3*

Long Life

For with thee is
the fountain of life:
in thy light shall
we see light.
Psalm 36:9

Thou wilt shew me the path of life: in thy presence is fulness of joy; at thy right hand there are pleasures for evermore.   *Psalm 16:11*

My times are in thy hand: deliver me from the hand of mine enemies, and from them that persecute me.
                                                    Psalm 31:15

What man is he that desireth life, and loveth many days, that he may see good? Keep thy tongue from evil, and thy lips from speaking guile. Depart from evil, and do good seek peace,and pursue it.
                                                Psalm 34:12-14

Depart from evil, and do good; and dwell for evermore. For the LORD loveth judgment, and forsaketh not his saints; they are preserved for ever: but the seed of the wicked shall be cut off.   *Psalm 37:27, 28*

Lord, make me to know mine end, and the measure of my days, what it is; that I may know how frail I am. Behold, thou hast made my days as an handbreadth; and mine age is as nothing before thee: verily every man at his best state is altogether vanity. Selah.
                                                    Psalm 39:4, 5

Cast thy burden upon the LORD, and he shall sustain thee; he shall never suffer the righteous to be moved. But thou, O God, shalt bring them down into the pit of destruction: bloody and deceitful men shall not live out half their days; but I will trust in thee.

Psalm 55:22, 23

Cast me not off in the time of old age; forsake me not when my strength faileth.   *Psalm 71:9*

O God, thou hast taught me from my youth: and hitherto have I declared thy wondrous works. Now also when I am old and greyheaded, O God, forsake me not; until I have shewed thy strength unto this generation, and thy power to every one that is to come.

Psalm 71:17, 18

With long life will I satisfy him, and shew him my salvation.   *Psalm 91:16*

Lust

For, lo,
they that are far
from thee shall perish:
thou hast destroyed all them
that go a whoring from thee.
But it is good for me
to draw near to God:
I have put my trust
in the Lord God,
that I may declare all thy works.
Psalm 73:27, 28

For the wicked boasteth of his heart's desire, and blesseth the covetous, whom the LORD abhorreth.

Psalm 10:3

Remember not the sins of my youth, nor my transgressions: according to thy mercy remember thou me
for thy goodness' sake, O LORD. Good and upright
is the LORD: therefore will he teach sinners in the
way.

Psalm 25:7, 8

Let them be confounded and put to shame that seek
after my soul: let them be turned back and brought to
confusion that devise my hurt.   *Psalm 35:4*

Bless the LORD, O my soul, and forget not all his ben-
efits: Who forgiveth all thine iniquities; who healeth
all thy diseases; who redeemeth thy life from destruction; who crowneth thee with lovingkindness and tender mercies; who satisfieth thy mouth with good
things; so that thy youth is renewed like the eagle's.

Psalm 103:2-5

Fools, because of their transgression, and because of their iniquities, are afflicted. Their soul abhorreth all manner of meat; and they draw near unto the gates of death. Then they cry unto the LORD in their trouble, and he saveth them out of their distresses. He sent his word, and healed them, and delivered them from their destructions. *Psalm 107:17-19*

Then shall I not be ashamed, when I have respect unto all thy commandments. *Psalm 119:6*

Wherewithal shall a young man cleanse his way? by taking heed thereto according to thy word.
Psalm 119:9

Patience

———✦———

Rest in the Lord,
and wait patiently for him:
fret not thyself because of him
who prospereth in his way,
because of the man who
bringeth wicked devices to pass.
Psalm 37:7

Yea, let none that wait on thee be ashamed: let them be ashamed which transgress without cause.

Psalm 25:3

Let integrity and uprightness preserve me; for I wait on thee. *Psalm 25:21*

Wait on the LORD: be of good courage, and he shall strengthen thine heart: wait, I say, on the LORD.

Psalm 27:14

Our soul waiteth for the LORD: he is our help and our shield. For our heart shall rejoice in him, because we have trusted in his holy name. *Psalm 33:20, 21*

Wait on the LORD, and keep his way, and he shall exalt thee to inherit the land: when the wicked are cut off, thou shalt see it. *Psalm 37:34*

I waited patiently for the LORD; and he inclined unto me, and heard my cry. *Psalm 40:1*

Truly my soul waiteth upon God: from him cometh my salvation. *Psalm 62:1*

My soul, wait thou only upon God; for my expectation is from him. He only is my rock and my salvation: he is my defence; I shall not be moved.

Psalm 62:5, 6

Thy testimonies have I taken as an heritage for ever: for they are the rejoicing of my heart. I have inclined mine heart to perform thy statutes always, even unto the end.

Psalm 119:111, 112

I wait for the LORD, my soul doth wait, and in his word do I hope. My soul waiteth for the LORD more than they that watch for the morning: I say, more than they that watch for the morning. Let Israel hope in the LORD: for with the LORD there is mercy, and with him is plenteous redemption. *Psalm 130:5-7*

The LORD taketh pleasure in them that fear him, in those that hope in his mercy. *Psalm 147:11*

Peace and Joy
(gifts of God)

I will both lay me down
in peace, and sleep:
for thou, Lord,
only makest me dwell in safety.
Psalm 4:8

Blessed is the man that walketh not in the counsel of the ungodly, nor standeth in the way of sinners, nor sitteth in the seat of the scornful. But his delight is in the law of the LORD; and in his law doth he meditate day and night. And he shall be like a tree planted by the rivers of water, that bringeth forth his fruit in his season; his leaf also shall not wither; and whatsoever he doeth shall prosper.   *Psalm 1:1-3*

Thou wilt shew me the path of life: in thy presence is fulness of joy; at thy right hand there are pleasures for evermore.   *Psalm 16:11*

The Lord is my shepherd; I shall not want. He maketh me to lie down in green pastures: he leadeth me beside the still waters. He restoreth my soul: he leadeth me in the paths of righteousness for his name's sake.
                          Psalm 23:1-3

What man is he that feareth the LORD? him shall he teach in the way that he shall choose. His soul shall dwell at ease; and his seed shall inherit the earth.
                          Psalm 25:12, 13

Thou hast turned for me my mourning into dancing: thou hast put off my sackcloth, and girded me with gladness; to the end that my glory may sing praise to thee, and not be silent. O LORD my God, I will give thanks unto thee for ever.   *Psalm 30:11, 12*

The young lions do lack, and suffer hunger: but they that seek the LORD shall not want any good thing.
                                        Psalm 34:10

But the meek shall inherit the earth; and shall delight themselves in the abundance of peace.   *Psalm 37:11*

The steps of a good man are ordered by the LORD: and he delighteth in his way. Though he fall, he shall not be utterly cast down: for the LORD upholdeth him with his hand.   *Psalm 37:23, 24*

Mark the perfect man, and behold the upright: for the end of that man is peace.   *Psalm 37:37*

Restore unto me the joy of thy salvation; and uphold me with thy free spirit.   *Psalm 51:12*

The Lord will give
strength unto his people;
the Lord will bless
his people with peace.
Psalm 29:11

He hath delivered my soul in peace from that battle that was against me: for there were many with me.

Psalm 55:18

Thus will I bless thee while I live: I will lift up my hands in thy name. My soul shall be satisfied as with marrow and fatness; and my mouth shall praise thee with joyful lips.

Psalm 63:4, 5

Thy way, O God, is in the sanctuary: who is so great a God as our God?

Psalm 77:13

For a day in thy courts is better than a thousand. I had rather be a doorkeeper in the house of my God, than to dwell in the tents of wickedness. For the LORD God is a sun and shield: the LORD will give grace and glory: no good thing will he withhold from them that walk uprightly. O LORD of hosts, blessed is the man that trusteth in thee.

Psalm 84:10-12

I will hear what God the LORD will speak: for he will speak peace unto his people, and to his saints: but let them not turn again to folly.

Psalm 85:8

Surely his salvation is nigh them that fear him; that glory may dwell in our land. Mercy and truth are met together; righteousness and peace have kissed each other. Truth shall spring out of the earth; and righteousness shall look down from heaven. Yea, the LORD shall give that which is good; and our land shall yield her increase.   *Psalm 85:9-12*

Blessed is the people that know the joyful sound: they shall walk, O LORD, in the light of thy countenance. In thy name shall they rejoice all the day: and in thy righteousness shall they be exalted.   *Psalm 89:15, 16*

For he is our God; and we are the people of his pasture, and the sheep of his hand.   *Psalm 95:7a*

This is the day which the LORD hath made; we will rejoice and be glad in it.   *Psalm 118:24*

Great peace have they which love thy law: and nothing shall offend them.   *Psalm 119:165*

I was glad when they said unto me, Let us go into the house of the LORD.   *Psalm 122:1*

Happy is that people,
that is in such a case:
yea, happy is that people,
whose God is the LORD.
Psalm 144:15

The LORD hath done great things for us; whereof we are glad. . .They that sow in tears shall reap in joy.

Psalm 126:3, 5

Blessed is every one that feareth the LORD; that walketh in his ways. For thou shalt eat the labour of thine hands: happy shalt thou be, and it shall be well with thee.

Psalm 128:1, 2

Behold, how good and how pleasant it is for brethren to dwell together in unity! *Psalm 133:1*

Poverty
(for those in need)

Blessed is he that
considereth the poor:
the LORD will deliver him
in time of trouble.
The LORD will preserve him,
and keep him alive;
and he shall be blessed
upon the earth:
and thou wilt not
deliver him unto the will
of his enemies.
Psalm 41:1, 2

For the needy shall not always be forgotten: the expectation of the poor shall not perish for ever. *Psalm 9:18*

Thou hast seen it; for thou beholdest mischief and spite, to requite it with thy hand: the poor committeth himself unto thee; thou art the helper of the fatherless.
Psalm 10:14

For the oppression of the poor, for the sighing of the needy, now will I arise, saith the Lord; I will set him in safety from him that puffeth at him. *Psalm 12:5*

As for me, I will behold thy face in righteousness: I shall be satisfied, when I awake, with thy likeness.
Psalm 17:15

The meek shall eat and be satisfied: they shall praise the LORD that seek him: your heart shall live for ever.
Psalm 22:26

They looked unto him, and were lightened: and their faces were not ashamed. This poor man cried, and the Lord heard him, and saved him out of all his troubles.
Psalm 34:5, 6

All my bones shall say, LORD, who is like unto thee, which deliverest the poor from him that is too strong for him, yea, the poor and the needy from him that spoileth him?   *Psalm 35:10*

The LORD knoweth the days of the upright: and their inheritance shall be for ever. They shall not be ashamed in the evil time: and in the days of famine they shall be satisfied.   *Psalm 37:18, 19*

But I am poor and needy; yet the LORD thinketh upon me: thou art my help and my deliverer; make no tarrying, O my God.   *Psalm 40:17*

A father of the fatherless, and a judge of the widows, is God in his holy habitation. God setteth the solitary in families: he bringeth out those which are bound with chains: but the rebellious dwell in a dry land.
Psalm 68:5, 6

Thy congregation hath dwelt therein: thou, O God, hast prepared of thy goodness for the poor.
Psalm 68:10

Happy is he that hath the God
of Jacob for his help,
whose hope is in the Lord his God:
which executeth judgment
or the oppressed:
which giveth food to the hungry.
The Lord looseth the prisoners:
the Lord openeth the eyes of the blind:
the Lord raiseth them
that are bowed down:
the Lord loveth the righteous:
the Lord preserveth the strangers;
he relieveth the fatherless and widow:
but the way of the wicked
he turneth upside down.
Psalm 146:5, 7-10

For he shall deliver the needy when he crieth, the poor also, and him that hath no helper. He shall spare the poor and needy, and shall save the souls of the needy. He shall redeem their soul from deceit and violence: and precious shall their blood be in his sight.   *Psalm 72:12-14*

He will regard the prayer of the destitute, and not despise their prayer.   *Psalm 102:17*

Oh, that men would praise the LORD for his goodness, and for his wonderful works to the children of men! For he satisfieth the longing soul, and filleth the hungry soul with goodness.   *Psalm 107:8, 9*

Yet setteth he the poor on high from affliction, and maketh him families like a flock.   *Psalm 107:41*

For he shall stand at the right hand of the poor, to save him from those that condemn his soul.
      Psalm 109:31

The LORD is gracious and full of compassion. He hath given meat unto them that fear him: he will ever be mindful of his covenant.   *Psalm 111:4b, 5*

He raiseth up the poor out of the dust, and lifteth the needy out of the dunghill; that he may set him with princes, even with the princes of his people.

Psalm 113:7, 8

The LORD preserveth the simple: I was brought low, and he helped me. For thou hast delivered my soul from death, mine eyes from tears, and my feet from falling. I will walk before the LORD in the land of the living.

Psalm 116:6, 8, 9

I will abundantly bless her provision: I will satisfy her poor with bread.   *Psalm 132:15*

I know that the LORD will maintain the cause of the afflicted, and the right of the poor. Surely the righteous shall give thanks unto thy name: the upright shall dwell in thy presence.   *Psalm 140:12, 13*

The LORD upholdeth all that fall, and raiseth up all those that be bowed down. The eyes of all wait upon thee; and thou givest them their meat in due season. Thou openest thine hand, and satisfiest the desire of every living thing. The LORD is righteous in all his ways, and holy in all his works.   *Psalm 145:14-17*

Prayer

And call upon me
in the day of trouble:
I will deliver thee,
and thou shalt glorify me.
Psalm 50:15

Hearken unto the voice of my cry, my King, and my God: for unto thee will I pray. My voice shalt thou hear in the morning, O LORD; in the morning will I direct my prayer unto thee, and will look up. For thou art not a God that hath pleasure in wickedness: neither shall evil dwell with thee. *Psalm 5:2-4*

I have called upon thee, for thou wilt hear me, O God: incline thine ear unto me, and hear my speech.
Psalm 17:6

I acknowledged my sin unto thee, and mine iniquity have I not hid. I said, I will confess my transgressions unto the LORD; and thou forgavest the iniquity of my sin. Selah. For this shall every one that is godly pray unto thee in a time when thou mayest be found: surely in the floods of great waters they shall not come nigh unto them. *Psalm 32:5, 6*

I sought the LORD, and he heard me, and delivered me from all my fears. They looked unto him, and were lightened: and their faces were not ashamed.
Psalm 34:4, 5

The righteous cry, and the LORD heareth, and delivereth them out of all their troubles. *Psalm 34:17*

As for me, I will call upon God; and the LORD shall save me. Evening, and morning, and at noon, will I pray, and cry aloud: and he shall hear my voice.
Psalm 55:16, 17

If I regard iniquity in my heart, the LORD will not hear me: But verily God hath heard me; he hath attended to the voice of my prayer. Blessed be God, which hath not turned away my prayer, nor his mercy from me.
Psalm 66:18-20

He shall call upon me, and I will answer him; I will be with him in trouble; I will deliver him, and honour him.
Psalm 91:15

It is a good thing to give thanks unto the Lord, and to sing praises unto thy name, O most High: to shew forth thy lovingkindness in the morning, and thy faithfulness every night. *Psalm 92:1, 2*

O thou that hearest prayer,
unto thee shall all flesh come.
Iniquities prevail against me;
as for our transgressions,
thou shalt purge them away.
Psalm 65:2, 3

I know, O LORD, that thy judgments are right, and that thou in faithfulness hast afflicted me. Let, I pray thee, thy merciful kindness be for my comfort, according to thy word unto thy servant.   *Psalm 119:75, 76*

Pray for the peace of Jerusalem: they shall prosper that love thee.   *Psalm 122:6*

In the day when I cried thou answeredst me, and strengthenedst me with strength in my soul.
                                                    Psalm 138:3

Let my prayer be set forth before thee as incense; and the lifting up of my hands as the evening sacrifice.
                                                    Psalm 141:2

The LORD is nigh unto all them that call upon him, to all that call upon him in truth. He will fulfil the desire of them that fear him: he also will hear their cry, and will save them.   *Psalm 145:18, 19*

Pride
(and the gift of Humility)

The meek will he
guide in judgment:
and the meek will he
teach his way.
Psalm 25:9

O ye sons of men, how long will ye turn my glory into shame? how long will ye love vanity, and seek after leasing? Selah. But know that the LORD hath set apart him that is godly for himself: the LORD will hear when I call unto him. Stand in awe, and sin not: commune with your own heart upon your bed, and be still. Selah.

Psalm 4:2-4

When I consider thy heavens, the work of thy fingers, the moon and the stars, which thou hast ordained: What is man, that thou art mindful of him? and the son of man, that thou visitest him? *Psalm 8:3, 4*

When he maketh inquisition for blood, he remembereth them: he forgetteth not the cry of the humble.

Psalm 9:12

The wicked in his pride doth persecute the poor. . . . For the wicked boasteth of his heart's desire, and blesseth the covetous, whom the LORD abhorreth. The wicked, through the pride of his countenance, will not seek after God: God is not in all his thoughts. *Psalm 10:2-4*

LORD, thou hast heard the desire of the humble: thou wilt prepare their heart, thou wilt cause thine ear to hear. *Psalm 10:17*

For thou wilt save the afflicted people; but wilt bring down high looks.   *Psalm 18:27*

Who shall ascend into the hill of the LORD? or who shall stand in his holy place? He that hath clean hands, and a pure heart; who hath not lifted up his soul unto vanity, nor sworn deceitfully.   *Psalm 24:3, 4*

Let not the foot of pride come against me, and let not the hand of the wicked remove me. There are the workers of iniquity fallen: they are cast down, and shall not be able to rise.   *Psalm 36:11, 12*

For yet a little while, and the wicked shall not be: yea, thou shalt diligently consider his place, and it shall not be. But the meek shall inherit the earth; and shall delight themselves in the abundance of peace.
                                        Psalm 37:10, 11

LORD, make me to know mine end, and the measure of my days, what it is; that I may know how frail I am. Behold, thou hast made my days as an handbreadth; and mine age is as nothing before thee: verily every man at his best state is altogether vanity. Selah.
                                        Psalm 39:4, 5

The meek shall
eat and be satisfied:
they shall praise the Lord
that seek him:
your heart shall live forever.
Psalm 22:26

Blessed is that man that maketh the Lord his trust, and respecteth not the proud, nor such as turn aside to lies.
Psalm 40:4

For thou desirest not sacrifice; else would I give it: thou delightest not in burnt-offering. The sacrifices of God are a broken spirit: a broken and a contrite heart, O God, thou wilt not despise.   *Psalm 51:17*

Thou hast rebuked the proud that are cursed, which do err from thy commandments.   *Psalm 119:21*

Though the LORD be high, yet hath he respect unto the lowly: but the proud he knoweth afar off.
Psalm 138:6

The LORD lifteth up the meek: he casteth the wicked down to the ground.   *Psalm 147:6*

For the Lord taketh pleasure in his people: he will beautify the meek with salvation.   *Psalm 149:4*

Lift not up your horn on high: speak not with a stiff neck. For promotion cometh neither from the east, nor from the west, nor from the south. But God is the judge: he putteth down one, and setteth up another.

Psalm 75:5-7

Prophecy
(what has happened
and what will be)

Yet have I set my king upon
my holy hill of Zion.
I will declare the decree:
the Lord hath said unto me,
Thou art my Son;
this day have I begotten thee.
Blessed are all they that
put their trust in him.
Psalm 2:6, 7, 12b

[REFERS TO THE COMING OF GOD'S SON,
JESUS CHRIST; *SEE* MATTHEW 3:17]

Great deliverance giveth he to his king; and sheweth mercy to his anointed, to David, and to his seed for evermore.   *Psalm 18:50*

[REFERS TO GOD'S SON, JESUS,
A DIRECT DESCENDANT OF DAVID]

They gaped upon me with their mouths, as a ravening and a roaring lion. I am poured out like water, and all my bones are out of joint: my heart is like wax; it is melted in the midst of my bowels. My strength is dried up like a potsherd. . .for dogs have compassed me: the assembly of the wicked have inclosed me: they pierced my hands and my feet. I may tell all my bones: they look and stare upon me. They part my garments among them, and cast lots upon my vesture.

Psalm 22:13-18

[PORTRAYS GRAPHICALLY THE
CRUCIFIXION OF JESUS CHRIST; *SEE* MATTHEW 27]

I will declare thy name unto my brethren: in the midst of the congregation will I praise thee. For he hath not despised nor abhorred the affliction of the afflicted; neither hath he hid his face from him; but when he cried unto him, he heard.   *Psalm 22:22. 24*

[REFERS TO THE RESURRECTION OF
JESUS CHRIST; *SEE* JOHN 20:17]

A seed shall serve him; it shall be accounted to the LORD for a generation. They shall come, and shall declare his righteousness unto a people that shall be born, that he hath done this.   *Psalm 22:30, 31*

[REFERS TO THE RESTORATION OF GOD'S KINGDOM
IN THE END TIMES; *SEE* 1 CORINTHIANS 15:23, 24]

I waited patiently for the LORD; and he inclined unto me, and heard my cry. He brought me up also out of an horrible pit, out of the miry clay, and set my feet upon a rock, and established my goings. And he hath put a new song in my mouth, even praise unto our God: many shall see it, and fear, and shall trust in the LORD.

Psalm 40:1-3

[REFERS TO THE RESURRECTION OF JESUS CHRIST,
WHO WAS RAISED FROM THE DEAD THREE DAYS AFTER
BEING CRUCIFIED, AN EVENT WITNESSED BY MANY]

God is gone up with a shout, the LORD with the sound of a trumpet.   *Psalm 47:5*

[REFERS TO THE SECOND COMING
OF JESUS CHRIST WHOSE ARRIVAL WILL BE
ANNOUNCED BY THE SOUND OF A TRUMPET;
SEE MATTHEW 24:31; 1 CORINTHIANS 15:52;
1 THESSALONIANS 4:16]

He shall subdue
the people under us,
and the nations under our feet.
He shall choose
our inheritance for us,
the excellency of Jacob
whom he loved. Selah.
Psalm 47:3, 4

[REFERS TO THE INHERITANCE OF ALL CHRISTIANS
WHO RECEIVE JESUS CHRIST AS THEIR SAVIOR;
SEE 1 PETER 1:3, 4]

Our God shall come, and shall not keep silence: a fire shall devour before him, and it shall be very tempestuous round about him. He shall call to the heavens from above, and to the earth, that he may judge his people. Gather my saints together unto me; those that have made a covenant with me by sacrifice. And the heavens shall declare his righteousness: for God is judge himself. Selah.   *Psalm 50:3-6*

[REFERS TO SECOND COMING OF JESUS CHRIST; *SEE* ACTS 1:9-11]

Let not them that wait on thee, O LORD God of hosts, be ashamed for my sake: let not those that seek thee be confounded for my sake, O God of Israel. Because for thy sake I have borne reproach; shame hath covered my face. I am become a stranger unto my brethren, and an alien unto my mother's children. For the zeal of thine house hath eaten me up; and the reproaches of them that reproached thee are fallen upon me. They gave me also gall for my meat; and in my thirst they gave me vinegar to drink. Let their table become a snare before them: and that which should have been for their welfare, let it become a trap. Let their eyes be darkened that they see not. . . .   *Psalm 69:6-9, 21-23*

[REFERS TO THE REJECTION OF GOD'S SON, JESUS CHRIST, AND HIS DEATH ON THE CROSS; *SEE* MATTHEW 26 AND 27]

Let their habitation be desolate; and let none dwell in their tents. Let them be blotted out of the book of the living, and not be written with the righteous.

Psalm 69:25, 28

[REFERS TO JUDAS ISCARIOT, WHO BETRAYED JESUS CHRIST AND THEN HANGED HIMSELF; *SEE* ACTS 1:20]

He shall have dominion also from sea to sea, and from the river unto the ends of the earth. They that dwell in the wilderness shall bow before him; and his enemies shall lick the dust. The kings of Tarshish and of the isles shall bring presents: the kings of Sheba and Seba shall offer gifts. Yea, all kings shall fall down before him: all nations shall serve him. For he shall deliver the needy when he crieth, the poor also, and him that hath no helper. He shall spare the poor and needy, and shall save the souls of the needy. He shall redeem their soul from deceit and violence: and precious shall their blood be in his sight.

Psalm 72:8-14

[REFERS TO THE ESTABLISHMENT OF THE ETERNAL KINGDOM WITH JESUS CHRIST AS THE HEAD; *SEE* REVELATION 5]

His name shall endure for ever: his name shall be continued as long as the sun: and men shall be blessed in him: all nations shall call him blessed. *Psalm 72:17*

[REFERS TO THE ETERNAL KINGDOM OF JESUS CHRIST]

The stone which
the builders refused is
become the head stone of the corner.
This is the Lord's doing;
it is marvellous in our eyes.
Psalm 118:22, 23

[REFERS TO JESUS CHRIST AS THE "STONE," OR
THE FOUNDATION OF THE CHURCH,
WHO WAS REJECTED BUT WILL ONE DAY BE EXALTED;
SEE 1 PETER 2:8]

For lo, thine enemies make a tumult: and they that hate thee have lifted up the head. They have taken crafty counsel against thy people, and consulted against thy hidden ones. They have said, Come, and let us cut them off from being a nation; that the name of Israel may be no more in remembrance. *Psalm 83:2-4*

[MAY REFER TO THE PRESENT-DAY SITUATION
IN THE MIDDLE EAST]

The LORD said unto my Lord, Sit thou at my right hand, until I make thine enemies thy footstool. The LORD shall send the rod of thy strength out of Zion: rule thou in the midst of thine enemies. The LORD hath sworn, and will not repent, Thou art a priest for ever after the order of Melchizedek. The LORD at thy right hand shall strike through kings in the day of his wrath. He shall judge among the heathen, he shall fill the places with the dead bodies; he shall wound the heads over many countries. He shall drink of the brook in the way: therefore shall he lift up the head. *Psalm 110:1, 2, 4-7*

[REFERS TO THE END TIMES WHEN JESUS CHRIST
WILL RULE THE WORLD; JESUS IS A PRIEST LIKE
MELCHIZEDEK SINCE HE HAS
NO BEGINNING AND PROMISES PEACE;
SEE 1 CORINTHIANS 15:25; HEBREWS 5:6]

O daughter of Babylon, who art to be destroyed; happy shall he be, that rewardeth thee as thou hast served us.
Psalm 137:8
[REFERS TO THE DESTRUCTION OF BABYLON
AS PREDICTED IN REVELATION 18-19]

The LORD doth build up Jerusalem: he gathereth together the outcasts of Israel.   *Psalm 147:2*
[JERUSALEM WILL BE THE SITE OF THE ETERNAL
KINGDOM OF JESUS CHRIST; *SEE* REVELATION 21]

The Lord hath made known his salvation: his right-eousness hath he openly shewed in the sight of the heathen. He hath remembered his mercy and his truth toward the house of Israel: all the ends of the earth have seen the salvation of our God.   *Psalm 98:2, 3*
[REFERS TO THE ADVENT OF JESUS CHRIST;
SEE LUKE 2:30, 31]

Sanctity of Life

Lo,
children are an heritage
of the Lord:
and the fruit of the womb
is his reward.
Psalm 127:3

But thou art he that took me out of the womb: thou didst make me hope when I was upon my mother's breasts. I was cast upon thee from the womb: thou art my God from my mother's belly.   *Psalm 22:9, 10*

Behold, I was shapen in iniquity; and in sin did my mother conceive me.   *Psalm 51:5*
    [You are a human life when you are formed.]

By thee have I been holden up from the womb: thou art he that took me out of my mother's bowels: my praise shall be continually of thee.   *Psalm 71:6*

Know ye that the Lord he is God: it is he that hath made us, and not we ourselves; we are his people, and the sheep of his pasture.   *Psalm 100:3*

Like as a father pitieth his children, so the Lord pitieth them that fear him. For he knoweth our frame; he remembereth that we are dust.   *Psalm 103:13, 14*

For thou hast possessed my reins: thou hast covered me in my mother's womb. I will praise thee; for I am fearfully and wonderfully made: marvellous are thy works; and that my soul knoweth right well. My substance was not hid from thee, when I was made in secret, and curiously wrought in the lowest parts of the earth. Thine eyes did see my substance, yet being unperfect; and in thy book all my members were written, which in continuance were fashioned, when as yet there was none of them.   *Psalm 139:13-16*

Wealth
(love of material goods)

A little that
a righteous man hath
is better than the riches
of many wicked.
Psalm 37:16

LORD, who shall abide in thy tabernacle? who shall dwell in thy holy hill?. . .He that putteth not out his money to usury, nor taketh reward against the innocent. He that doeth these things shall never be moved.

Psalm 15:1, 5

Some trust in chariots, and some in horses: but we will remember the name of the LORD our God. They are brought down and fallen: but we are risen, and stand upright. *Psalm 20:7, 8*

The young lions do lack, and suffer hunger: but they that seek the LORD shall not want any good thing.

Psalm 34:10

Rest in the LORD, and wait patiently for him: fret not thyself because of him who prospereth in his way, because of the man who bringeth wicked devices to pass.

Psalm 37:7

The LORD knoweth the days of the upright: and their inheritance shall be for ever. *Psalm 37:18*

The wicked borroweth, and payeth not again: but the righteous sheweth mercy, and giveth.   *Psalm 37:21*

Surely every man walketh in a vain shew: surely they are disquieted in vain: he heapeth up riches, and knoweth not who shall gather them.   *Psalm 39:6*

Wherefore should I fear in the days of evil, when the iniquity of my heels shall compass me about? They that trust in their wealth, and boast themselves in the multitude of their riches; none of them can by any means redeem his brother, nor give to God a ransom for him.
    Psalm 49:5-7

. . .Wise men die, likewise the fool and the brutish person perish, and leave their wealth to others. Their inward thought is, that their houses shall continue for ever, and their dwelling places to all generations; they call their lands after their own names. . . .This their way is their folly: yet their posterity approve their sayings. Selah.   *Psalm 49:10, 11, 13*

Be not thou afraid
when one is made rich,
when the glory of
his house is increased;
for when he dieth
he shall carry nothing away:
his glory shall not
descend after him.
Though while he lived
he blessed his soul:
and men will praise thee,
when thou doest well to thyself.
He shall go to
the generation of his fathers;
they shall never see light.
Man that is in honour,
and understandeth not,
is like the beasts that perish.
Psalm 49:16-20

Surely men of low degree are vanity, and men of high degree are a lie: to be laid in the balance, they are altogether lighter than vanity. Trust not in oppression, and become not vain in robbery: if riches increase, set not your heart upon them.   *Psalm 62:9, 10*

And they say, How doth God know? and is there knowledge in the most High? Behold, these are the ungodly, who prosper in the world; they increase in riches.
                                             Psalm 73:11, 12

A good man sheweth favour, and lendeth: he will guide his affairs with discretion. Surely he shall not be moved for ever: the righteous shall be in everlasting remembrance. He hath dispersed, he hath given to the poor; his righteousness endureth for ever; his horn shall be exalted with honour.   *Psalm 112:5, 6, 9*
I have rejoiced in the way of thy testimonies, as much as in all riches.   *Psalm 119:14*

Wisdom

The law of the Lord is perfect,
converting the soul:
the testimony of
the Lord is sure,
making wise the simple.
Psalm 19:7

Blessed is the man that walketh not in the counsel of the ungodly, nor standeth in the way of sinners, nor sitteth in the seat of the scornful. But his delight is in the law of the LORD; and in his law doth he meditate day and night. And he shall be like a tree planted by the rivers of water, that bringeth forth his fruit in his season; his leaf also shall not wither; and whatsoever he doeth shall prosper. *Psalm 1:1-3*

The fool hath said in his heart, There is no God. . . .The LORD looked down from heaven upon the children of men, to see if there were any that did understand, and seek God. *Psalm 14:1, 2*

I will bless the LORD, who hath given me counsel: my reins also instruct me in the night seasons. I have set the LORD always before me: because he is at my right hand, I shall not be moved. *Psalm 16:7, 8*

What man is he that feareth the LORD? him shall he teach in the way that he shall choose. His soul shall dwell at ease; and his seed shall inherit the earth. The secret of the LORD is with them that fear him; and he will shew them his covenant. *Psalm 25:12-14*

I will instruct thee and teach thee in the way which thou shalt go: I will guide thee with mine eye.

Psalm 32:8

Behold, thou desirest truth in the inward parts: and in the hidden part thou shalt make me to know wisdom.

Psalm 51:6

The fool hath said in his heart, There is no God. Corrupt are they, and have done abominable iniquity: there is none that doeth good.   _Psalm 53:1_

So teach us to number our days, that we may apply our hearts unto wisdom.   _Psalm 90:12_

O LORD, how great are thy works! and thy thoughts are very deep. A brutish man knoweth not; neither doth a fool understand this. When the wicked spring as the grass, and when all the workers of iniquity do flourish; it is that they shall be destroyed for ever: But thou, LORD, art most high for evermore.   _Psalm 92:5-8_

O Lord, how manifold are thy works! in wisdom hast thou made them all: the earth is full of thy riches.

Psalm 104:24

Whoso is wise, and will observe these things, even they shall understand the lovingkindness of the Lord.

Psalm 107:43

The fear of the Lord is the beginning of wisdom: a good understanding have all they that do his commandments: his praise endureth for ever.   *Psalm 111:10*

Thou through thy commandments hast made me wiser than mine enemies: for they are ever with me. I have more understanding than all my teachers: for thy testimonies are my meditation. I understand more than the ancients, because I keep thy precepts.

Psalm 119:98-100

The entrance of thy words giveth light; it giveth understanding unto the simple.   *Psalm 119:130*